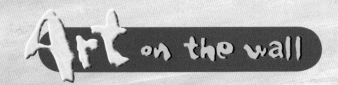

IMPRESSIONISM

Jane Bingham

Heinemann
LIBRARY

www.heinemann.co.uk/library

Visit our website to find out more information about Heinemann Library books.

To order:

 Phone 44 (0) 1865 888112

 Send a fax to 44 (0) 1865 314091

Visit the Heinemann bookshop at www.heinemann.co.uk/library to browse our catalogue and order online.

Produced for Heinemann Library by White-Thomson Publishing Ltd, Bridgewater Business Centre, 210 High Street, Lewes, East Sussex BN7 2NH.

Heinemann Library is an imprint of **Pearson Education Limited**, a company incorporated in England and Wales having its registered office at Edinburgh Gate, Harlow, Essex, CM20 2JE – Registered company number: 00872828 Heinemann is a registered trademark of Pearson Education Limited.

Text © Pearson Education Limited 2009
First published in hardback in 2009.
The moral rights of the proprietor have been asserted.

Edited by Clare Collinson and Megan Cotugno
Designed by Mayer Media Ltd
Picture research by Amy Sparks and Clare Collinson
Originated by Chroma Graphics
Printed and bound in China by Leo Paper Products

ISBN 978 0 431933 25 2 (hardback)
13 12 11 10 09
10 9 8 7 6 5 4 3 2 1

British Library Cataloguing in Publication Data

Bingham, Jane
Impressionism. - (Art on the wall)
1. Impressionism (Art) - Juvenile literature
I. Title
709'.0344

Acknowledgements

We would like to thank the following for permission to reproduce photographs:
Bridgeman Art Library **pp. 5** (National Gallery, London), **6** (Louvre, Paris/Giraudon), **7** (Wallace Collection, London), **8** (Private Collection/Lefevre Fine Art Ltd, London), **10** (Museus Castro Maya, Rio de Janeiro, Brazil), **11** (Samuel Courtauld Trust, Courtauld Institute of Art Gallery), **13** (Petit Palais, Geneva, Switzerland), **14** (National Gallery, London), **16–17** (Musée des Beaux-Arts, Lille, France/Lauros/Giraudon), 18 (Musée Marmottan, Paris/Giraudon), **19** (Samuel Courtauld Trust, Courtauld Institute of Art Gallery), **21** (National Gallery, London), **23** (Musée d'Orsay, Paris, Lauros/Giraudon), **24** (National Gallery, London), **25** (Allen Memorial Art Museum, Oberlin College, Ohio/R.T. Miller, Jr. Fund), **28** (Musée d'Orsay, Paris/Giraudon), **29** (Neue Pinakothek, Munich), **30** (Pushkin Museum, Moscow, Russia), **32** (Musée d'Orsay, Paris, France, Giraudon), **34** (Private Collection/Christie's Images), **35** (Private Collection), **36–37** (Fitzwilliam Museum, University of Cambridge); Corbis **pp. 26** (Burstein Collection), **39** (Philadelphia Museum of Art).

Cover photograph: Edgar Degas, *Blue Dancers* (c.1899), reproduced with permission of Bridgeman Art Library (Pushkin Museum, Moscow, Russia).

We would like to thank John Glaves-Smith for his invaluable help in the preparation of this book. We would also like to thank the staff and pupils of Headington School, Oxford, for their help in creating the artworks on pages 20 (Palita Rompotiyoke), 22 (Katrina Galsworthy), and 31 (Ann Chih).

Every effort has been made to contact copyright holders of material reproduced in this book. Any omissions will be rectified in subsequent printings if notice is given to the publishers.

Blue.

707.03
IMP

Contents

Some words are printed in bold, **like this.** You can find out what they mean by looking in the glossary.

What is Impressionism?

Look at the painting on page 5. It is by Monet, one of the leading members of the **Impressionist movement**. Can you see the glitter of the sunlight on the water? Do you sense the motion of the rowing boats bobbing up and down? And can you imagine the laughter of the bathers? These impressions – of light, movement, and noise – are all created by the artist. There is a sense that the artist has captured a single moment of life – and that is exactly what Monet aimed to do.

In the summer of 1869, Claude Monet and Pierre-Auguste Renoir painted a series of scenes at La Grenouillère, a popular bathing place on the banks of the River Seine near Paris, France. Monet and Renoir aimed to capture the lively atmosphere of the riverbank in their paintings. They worked in the open air, directly in front of their **subjects**. During the course of the summer, the two young artists experimented with new methods of painting, using strong, bright colours, and short, bold brushstrokes. Later, the style they developed was called Impressionism.

Who were the Impressionists?

The Impressionist movement began in France in the late 1860s and lasted until the opening years of the 20th century. Many artists are known as Impressionists, but the most famous were Monet, Renoir, Edgar Degas, Édouard Manet, Alfred Sisley, Paul Cèzanne, Camille Pissarro, and Berthe Morisot. They had their own individual styles and techniques, but they were united in their aim to adopt a new approach to art.

Taking it further

Reading this book will help you look at "art on the wall" in a new way. It will also give you suggestions for developing your own painting style. On pages 46–47, there are ideas for how to take your studies further and details of websites where you can view paintings by Impressionist artists.

Gaining a name

The Impressionists did not gain their name until 1874. In that year, the first of eight **Impressionist exhibitions** was held. It included a painting called *Impression: Sunrise* by Monet (see page 18). An **art critic** published a very negative review of the exhibition entitled "The Exhibition of the Impressionists". The artists tried to reject this title, but the name stuck.

Try it yourself

This book takes a close look at the styles and techniques of the Impressionist painters. It also gives you the chance to try out their techniques. Look out for the "Try it yourself" panels, and have a go at creating your own Impressionist images.

Claude Monet, *Bathers at La Grenouillère* (1869). This painting dates from the very creative period when Monet and Renoir were developing their new style. It shows one of the Impressionists' favourite subjects – people enjoying their leisure time.

A new kind of art

There are many reasons why Impressionism emerged in the 1860s. Firstly, the Impressionists reacted strongly against the popular painting style of their period. They were encouraged by the work of a few adventurous artists, who inspired them to adopt a fresh approach. The Impressionists also responded to the many **social** changes that were taking place in France in the second half of the 19th century.

The Paris Salon

In the mid-19th century, artists in France could only become successful if they showed their paintings at an annual art exhibition known as the **Salon**.

The paintings were selected by a jury made up of members of the French **Academy of Fine Arts**. The Academy had strict rules about the kind of paintings they would accept and almost always chose works by **academic** artists.

Academic art

Academic art had its origins in Italian painting of the 1500s. It is highly realistic and involves close attention to detail, fine brushwork, and a smooth finish. Academic artists usually worked in **studios**. They painted scenes from history, from the Bible, or from Greek and Roman mythology. They also painted portraits of wealthy people dressed in their finest clothes.

Charles Gleyre, *Lost Illusions or Evening* (1843). This painting is typical of the works that were exhibited at the Paris Salon. Painted in the academic style, it shows a poet on the banks of a river and a boat full of young women — a subject far removed from the everyday life of the French working people.

Theodore Rousseau, *The Forest at Fontainebleau: Morning* (1849–51). In spite of Rousseau's skill as a painter, his works were constantly rejected by the Paris Salon.

Art in the open air

Painting out of doors became much easier after the development of portable painting equipment and materials. In particular, the invention of metal paint tubes in 1841 meant that artists could work outside, with tubes of pre-mixed paints, instead of having to mix paint and oil in their studios.

Many outstanding artists painted in the academic style, but by the mid-19th century most academic painters were very unadventurous. However, a few **innovative** artists were determined to reject the strict rules of the Academy and adopt a new style of art.

The Barbizon School

One group of adventurous artists was known as the **Barbizon School**. This group was led by Theodore Rousseau, Charles-François Daubigny, and Camille Corot. In the 1840s, these artists moved to the village of Barbizon, near the Forest of Fontainebleau, south of Paris. There, they concentrated on **landscape painting**.

The Barbizon artists pioneered the practice of working out of doors, known as **plein-air painting**. They often painted the same scene again and again, in an attempt to capture the effects of light at different times of day. They also used brighter, lighter colours than artists had used before. The style and techniques of the Barbizon artists had an important influence on the emerging group of Impressionist artists.

French Realists

While the painters of the Barbizon School concentrated on landscape painting, another group of artists were showing a very different aspect of the French countryside – the everyday lives of French peasants. These artists became known as the **French Realists**. Through their paintings, they aimed to show that the lives of poor people, hard at work in the fields or at home in their villages, could be a suitable subject for art.

Among the leading French Realists were Jean-François Millet and Gustave Courbet. The Realists' choice of real-life subjects had a strong influence on the Impressionists. In particular, Pissarro produced some powerful studies of poor, working people.

Boudin at the seaside

One artist who had an influence on the Impressionists in the early years of the movement was the painter Eugène Boudin. He lived on the coast of Normandy in northern France, and painted dramatic landscapes and beach scenes, often showing stormy seas and skies. Boudin was a passionate believer in painting out of doors.

Eugène Boudin, *Beach Scene Near Trouville* (c.1863–66). Boudin was a skilful landscape painter who was greatly admired as "a master of the skies". He also managed to capture the jaunty mood of the holidaymakers.

By the 1850s, the coastal towns of Normandy had become popular holiday resorts. Throughout the summer months, families and friends arrived by train from Paris to enjoy themselves by the sea.

Boudin often painted these fashionable, smartly dressed figures, sitting together on the windswept beaches or strolling along the seashore holding their parasols. He often included large groups of people and developed a vivid, sketchy style to convey a sense of bustle, excitement, and colour.

Boudin and Monet

In 1858 Boudin became friends with the 18-year-old Monet and persuaded him to concentrate on developing his painting.

Monet was already a talented creator of **caricatures**, and under Boudin's guidance he learned to paint landscapes. Monet started working out of doors, painting directly from nature in all types of weather. He also made rapid sketches of people.

Boudin helped Monet to paint the changing effects of light on water, and to notice how the sky changed in different kinds of weather. Boudin also introduced Monet to one of the main subjects of Impressionist paintings – families and friends enjoying their leisure time.

Boudin's advice

Boudin urged Monet to paint out of doors whenever he could. He believed that this was the only way to create bold and confident paintings.

"Everything painted directly and on the spot has a strength, vigour, and vivacity of touch that can never be attained in a studio; three brushstrokes from nature are worth more than two days' studio work at the easel."
Eugène Boudin

Try it yourself

Painting on the spot
When you paint directly in front of the subject you are depicting, you learn to look at things much more carefully than when you paint from memory. Try making lots of rapid sketches of an object or scene you observe, either in pencils or in paint. Don't aim to create a masterpiece. Instead, show exactly what you see in terms of light, colour, and shapes.

Constable and Turner

The work of two British artists had an influence on the development of the Impressionist style. The landscape painter John Constable worked in England in the early 19th century and specialized in painting scenes of country life. He was very interested in capturing the effects of light on a landscape. Constable's work was greatly admired in France, especially by the artists of the Barbizon School. They used some of Constable's techniques in their landscape paintings and they in turn influenced the Impressionists.

Another English landscape artist, J.M.W. Turner, had a long painting career, which lasted until the 1850s. Turner was famous for his dramatic landscapes. He was especially interested in capturing the effects of light, and in showing weather conditions such as rain and fog. Monet and Pissarro studied paintings by Constable and Turner in the National Gallery in London while they were staying in England in the early 1870s.

Hiroshige, *The Banks of the Omaya* (1857). Japanese prints caused great excitement among the Impressionists because they did not obey the "rules" of Western art.

Inspiration from Japan

In the 1860s, **woodblock prints** from Japan became very popular in France. Japanese printmakers such as Hiroshige and Hokusai used large blocks of strong, **flat colour** contrasting with areas of intricate pattern. Their paintings often had no single **point of focus** and they created striking **asymmetrical compositions**, in which the main subject is placed off centre. They also showed their subjects from unusual viewpoints and framed their paintings in exciting ways, sometimes cutting off parts of their subjects at the edge of the picture. Manet, Degas, Monet, and the U.S.-born Impressionist Mary Cassatt were all strongly influenced by the work of Japanese printmakers (see also pages 24–25).

Influence of photography

The process of photography was first developed in the first half of the 19th century. By the 1860s, photographers were producing photographic portraits and sepia (brown and white) images of landscapes. Some people predicted that photography would take over from painting as a way of recording the world. However, the Impressionists did not see photography as a threat. Instead, they believed that it freed them from having to produce an accurate record of the world around them, and allowed them to create their own impressions of a scene.

New scientific ideas

During the 19th century, scientific knowledge was advancing very rapidly and there was an explosion of interest in scientific ideas. People were especially fascinated by the study of **optics**. Scientific toys that demonstrated how people see light and colour were very popular. The Impressionists kept up with all the latest theories about light and colour, and used these ideas in the development of their painting techniques (see pages 22–23).

Claude Monet, *Antibes* (1888). Look at the way this picture is composed and framed. Can you see the influence of the Japanese printmakers on Monet's art?

Changes in society

The Impressionists were strongly influenced by the dramatic changes taking place in French society. By the 1860s, life in many parts of France was changing fast. The **Industrial Revolution**, which had begun in England in the 1750s, had quickly spread to France. During the first half of the 19th century, hundreds of factories were built, and towns and cities grew rapidly.

While people in the countryside still worked in the fields, men and women in cities and towns were employed in factories, shops, and offices. These new workers had money to spend and leisure time to enjoy. People began to gather after work in public parks, cafés, and bars. They visited the theatre and the ballet. They went bathing and boating on the river, and they took trips to the seaside, often travelling by train.

Modern Paris

The most dramatic changes in the French way of life took place in Paris. In less than 20 years, between 1852 and 1870, the French capital was transformed. Napoleon III, who ruled France as emperor, gave orders that the medieval city centre should be replaced with wide streets, squares, and tree-filled parks.

The architect of the new Paris was Baron Haussmann. He designed a network of avenues, known as boulevards. There were wide pavements, where people could stroll easily, and broad roads to allow plenty of room for carriages. The newly designed city also had many cafés where people could gather by day and night.

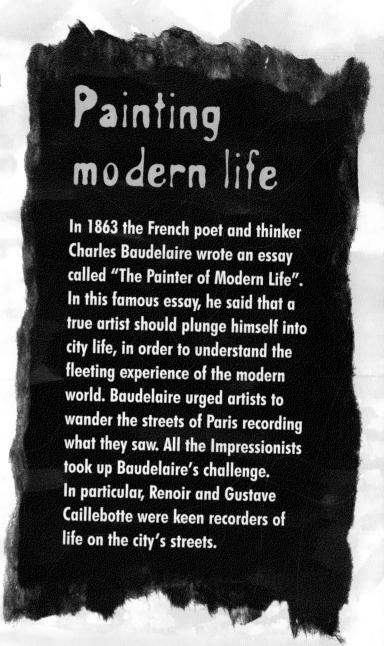

Painting modern life

In 1863 the French poet and thinker Charles Baudelaire wrote an essay called "The Painter of Modern Life". In this famous essay, he said that a true artist should plunge himself into city life, in order to understand the fleeting experience of the modern world. Baudelaire urged artists to wander the streets of Paris recording what they saw. All the Impressionists took up Baudelaire's challenge. In particular, Renoir and Gustave Caillebotte were keen recorders of life on the city's streets.

Haussmann also built five major railway stations in the city. This made it easy to travel to and from Paris in any direction. Families often took a train to the coast or countryside, or visited one of the newly created parks on the outskirts of the city. The Impressionists themselves also regularly travelled by train to visit the outer suburbs and the countryside.

The modern city of Paris was a central theme in much Impressionist art (see pages 28–29).

Try it yourself

Snapshots of the city

In their images of Paris, the Impressionists aimed to capture a moment of city life. Their pictures are not posed and the people are hurrying past, busy with their own lives. Why not try using a camera to capture a busy moment in people's lives? It doesn't matter if you don't live in a city. You can still take photos of people passing by on a street.

Gustave Caillebotte, *Le Pont de l'Europe* (1876). Like many of the Impressionists, Caillebotte was fascinated by the changing face of Paris. This painting features a modern railway bridge, while in the distance the buildings and boulevards of Haussmann's remodelled city can be seen.

The story of the movement

The Impressionist movement had its origins in the early 1860s in Paris, when a group of young artists began to experiment with new ways of painting. Over the next 20 years, these artists managed to change the face of the art world for ever.

Early meetings

In 1862 the 22-year-old Monet began to study with the painter Charles Gleyre in Paris. By that time, Monet had known Boudin for four years, and had developed a distinctive method of painting landscapes peopled with figures.

Gleyre was a member of the French Academy of Fine Arts, who painted in the academic style. However, his classes were very cheap and he allowed his pupils a lot of freedom. At Gleyre's studio, Monet met three more art students who were in their early twenties – Renoir, Sisley, and Frédéric Bazille. The four young men all began to experiment with new ways of painting, in a lighter, freer style.

The four artists soon widened their group of friends to include Cézanne, Pissarro, and Morisot. Berthe Morisot had studied with Corot, one of the Barbizon School artists.

Morisot was a great enthusiast for open-air painting. Cézanne was interested in showing real-life scenes and in trying out new painting techniques. Camille Pissarro was in his thirties – older than most of the group. Nevertheless, he still shared their ambition to produce a newer, fresher kind of art.

Degas and Manet

During the 1860s, two other painters were developing their own highly individual styles. Degas painted scenes of cafés and racecourses, using areas of strong, bright colour. Manet worked in a style that was partly influenced by Japanese art. He used vivid colours and was especially fond of scarlet and turquoise-green.

Frédéric Bazille

Frédéric Bazille was a key member of the Impressionist movement in its very early years. He came from a wealthy family and had started to train as a doctor before abandoning medicine to pursue his passion for art. His artistic career came to a sudden end in 1870, when he was killed fighting for the French in the **Franco-Prussian War** (see page 19).

Modern-life subjects

In the early 1860s, Manet began to paint scenes of modern city life. In 1862 he produced *Music in the Tuileries Gardens*, which has been described as one of the earliest Impressionist paintings. The painting shows a lively crowd of people who have gathered for a concert in a park in central Paris.

Music in the Tuileries Gardens looks very different from the work of the academic French artists of the time. Not only does it show "ordinary" people enjoying their everyday life and leisure time, but the brushwork lacks the smooth finish normally found in paintings at the time. The **composition** of the painting also has no central point of focus.

Manet's bold new technique and his choice of modern-life subject matter had a great influence on the other emerging Impressionist artists.

Édouard Manet, *Music in the Tuileries Gardens* (1862). In this painting Manet attempted to show modern life in a bold new style. He included a portrait of himself (on the extreme left of the painting) and of his artist friends. Also shown in the scene is the critic and poet Baudelaire, who was famous for his views on the importance of representing modern life in art.

Rejection by the Salon

During the 1860s, the group of emerging Impressionist artists tried to have their paintings shown in the Paris Salon, the annual art exhibition organized by the French Academy of Fine Arts. This exhibition was the best chance for the artists to gain recognition, get publicity, and sell their paintings. However, the Salon jury favoured the work of artists who painted in the academic style. Artists who painted in a "modern" style stood almost no chance at all. The young artists had some of their less adventurous paintings exhibited, but many of their works were rejected.

The Salon des Refusés

In 1863 the Salon jury rejected Manet's painting *Luncheon on the Grass*. This painting shows two men wearing contemporary dress, sitting at a picnic on the grass with a woman who is nude. The Salon exhibitions often included paintings showing idealized nudes in a historical, religious, or mythological setting, but the jury condemned Manet for placing a realistic nude in a modern scene. The jury's sharply worded rejection of Manet's painting, along with the unusually large number of rejected works that year, caused a storm of protest among French artists.

Eventually, the protest attracted the attention of the French ruler, Napoleon III. He gave his permission for an exhibition to be organized that would show the works that had been turned down by the Salon jury. This exhibition was known as the **Salon des Refusés**, and it gave critics, **art dealers**, and the public a rare chance to view some modern works. Although many visitors simply came to mock, the Salon des Refusés attracted larger crowds than the Paris Salon.

Alfred Sisley, *Port Marly, White Frost* (1872). Sisley was an early member of the Impressionist group. He was especially interested in the colours found in reflections and shadows. This painting explores the dramatic visual effects of frost on a landscape.

Struggling artists

The Salon des Refusés helped to publicize the work of the Impressionists and it introduced their new, modern painting style to more people. However, frequent rejections from the Salon in the years that followed meant that the emerging Impressionists still found their works difficult to sell and many of the young artists struggled with poverty.

A new style develops

Despite many difficulties, the artists continued to experiment with new ways of painting. They made frequent visits to the French countryside, where they painted outdoors whenever they could, and they also painted lively scenes of Paris and its suburbs.

In the summer of 1869, Monet and Renoir painted together, working side by side on the riverbank at La Grenouillère (see page 4). This was a crucial time for the two artists. By the end of the summer they had produced an exciting series of paintings in the bold new style, which would later be called Impressionism.

Try it yourself

Shadow study
While they were painting at La Grenouillère, Monet and Renoir studied light and shade very carefully. They noticed that shadows are not brown or black but are coloured by their surroundings. Look at the shadows cast by a tree on a sunny day. What colours can you see in them? (You might find that the shadows look purple or blue.) Could you show these colours in paint? Don't use black to make your colours darker, but try using different mixtures of blue and red to create a range of blue and purple shadows.

Claude Monet, *Impression: Sunrise* (1872). This painting was included in the first Impressionist exhibition. Its title may have been what led the critics to give the group their name (see page 4).

First Impressionist exhibition

By the 1870s, the Impressionists were desperate for somewhere to show their paintings. Without an exhibition, it was difficult to attract the attention of the art dealers who might buy their work. Eventually, they decided they would have to hold an exhibition of their own, and, in 1874, Monet organized an exhibition in the Paris studio of the photographer Nadar.

In total, 30 artists took part in the first Impressionist exhibition, including Monet, Renoir, Pissarro, Sisley, Cézanne, Morisot, and Degas. Manet refused to exhibit his paintings, insisting that the only true testing ground for his work was the Paris Salon.

Challenging times

The first Impressionist exhibition was not a **commercial** success and the art critics wrote damning reviews. The following years continued to be difficult, as the Impressionists tried to sell their works. However, despite these setbacks, they gradually attracted some loyal collectors.

Gaining popularity

In the 1870s, the French art dealer Paul Durand-Ruel began to sell the Impressionists' work, and he promoted their paintings in Paris, London, and New York. The wealthy artist Caillebotte also supported his fellow painters by buying their works and sponsoring their exhibitions.

In 1876 the Impressionists held a second exhibition, and over the next 10 years there were six more exhibitions devoted to Impressionist art. Art collectors continued to buy their works and their paintings became more popular with the general public.

Different directions

The last Impressionist exhibition was held in 1886. By this time, the shared aims that had kept the group together for almost 20 years had begun to vanish. The Impressionist artists no longer worked closely together and they began to follow their own artistic directions (see page 38). By the 1920s, most of the original group had either died or changed their style of painting. With Monet's death in 1926, the Impressionist movement finally came to an end, although its influence continues right up to the present day.

War in France

In 1870 war broke out between France and Prussia. At that time Prussia was the leading state in the vast German Empire and it was keen to seize French territory. In September 1870 Prussian troops invaded Paris. Monet, Pissarro, and Sisley all escaped to England, where they continued to paint. But most of the other Impressionists joined the French army, and Bazille was killed in battle. The war lasted for a year and when it was over the Impressionists gradually gathered again in Paris.

Camille Pissarro, *Lordship Lane Station, Dulwich* (1871). This picture was painted while Pissarro was living in London. Unlike most artists of the time, the Impressionists believed that suburban houses and railway trains were suitable subjects for a painting.

Impressionist techniques

The Impressionists developed a very distinctive style of painting. They pioneered daring new brushwork techniques and developed a new way of using colour. They also adopted a new approach to composition, painting scenes from unusual viewpoints and framing their subjects in exciting ways.

Brushwork techniques

In order to convey the sense of light and movement they observed in nature, the Impressionists experimented with different kinds of brushstrokes. They used a much looser style than academic painters, with clearly visible brushstrokes.

Monet and Renoir developed a technique of applying many small dabs of separate colour. These short strokes of paint are sometimes known as **taches**. They create a lively surface that appears to sparkle with reflected light. The method of using small *taches* of paint was adopted by most of the Impressionists in the early years of the movement, but gradually artists developed their own individual brushwork techniques.

Cézanne's technique

Cézanne created a very individual style of painting in order to show light and shade in a landscape. He applied his paint in patches of colour, using lots of diagonal brushstrokes very close together. In some of his paintings, he used a **palette knife** to achieve a patchy effect, applying his paint in thick slabs of colour.

Try it yourself

Brushstroke challenge

Why not try to paint a picture using lots of small, bold brushstrokes or *taches*? You will need a medium-sized brush and some thick paint – either oil or acrylic. This brushwork technique works especially well for images of water.

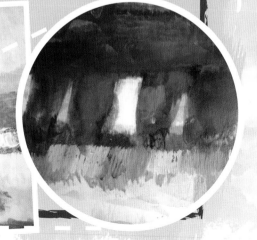

In this painting, a teenage artist has created a great effect using short strokes of varied colours.

A new approach to colour

The Impressionists noted the many different colours that can be seen in the natural world, for example in a pool of water, or a cloud. They also noticed how the colour of an object can change depending on the colours surrounding it and the light in which it is seen. The artists aimed to reflect their new understanding of the natural world by their adventurous use of colour.

The Impressionists tried to restrict themselves to colours that had been made by mixing the three **primary colours** of yellow, red, and blue. They kept their **palette** light and bright by avoiding mixing colours with black or brown. Monet, Renoir, and Sisley used a lot of white for highlights. Most of the Impressionists avoided black altogether, but some of them used it sparingly to create a dramatic effect.

Pierre-Auguste Renoir, *Boating on the Seine* (c.1879). In this painting, Renoir uses bright colours and plenty of white, with just a few touches of black for contrast. Notice how the *taches* of varied coloured paint create the effect of light sparkling on the water.

Try it yourself

Colour wheel

Each of the three primary colours – red, yellow, and blue – has a complementary colour, which is made by mixing together the other two primary colours. On a **colour wheel**, complementary colours are shown opposite each other.

Try painting your own simple colour wheel. Use only the primary colours, mixing them to make the secondary colours. On a sheet of paper draw a circle. Divide the circle into six equal parts and colour each part in the following order – blue, purple, red, orange, yellow, and green. You can use the colour wheel for reference to help you create some vibrant contrasts in your own paintings.

A colour wheel, showing the three primary colours opposite their complementary colours.

Complementary colours

The Impressionists were very interested in ideas about the way the eyes perceive colour and light. In particular, they created some striking effects through the use of **complementary colours**.

Complementary colours are direct opposites of each other (for example, red and green, and blue and orange). When two complementary colours are placed side by side, the colours appear brighter and stronger. The green looks more intensely green and the red appears to be a more vivid red.

The Impressionists often used complementary colours to capture the vibrant effects of light and colour they observed in nature. Cézanne and Pissarro were especially fond of using red and green next to each other, while Renoir and Monet often put orange and blue side by side. The Impressionists also used complementary colours to create dramatic shadows. For example, orange-coloured trees might be shown with blue shadows.

Optical mixing

The Impressionists also noticed that when very fine brushstrokes of different colours are placed close together, the colours appear from a distance to mix together, forming another shade. This visual effect is known as **optical mixing**, because the mixing happens in the eyes and brain, rather than on the **canvas**.

Monet was especially interested in the effects of optical mixing. He continued to experiment all his life, using lots of different colours close together to create a dappled, shimmering effect (see his painting, *Haystack*, on page 26). However, the artist who took these ideas one stage further was Georges Seurat (see panel).

Seurat and painting by dots

In the 1880s, Seurat created a technique of making paintings entirely from coloured dots. Seurat's works rely on the process of optical mixing. When viewed close up, his paintings are simply thousands of tiny dots of colour, placed side by side. However, when they are viewed from a distance, the dots mix together to form a scene. Seurat's style of painting is sometimes known as **pointillism** (see also page 39).

Japanese style

Some Impressionist painters were clearly influenced by the style and approach of Japanese printmakers (see page 10). For example, Degas, Renoir, and Cassatt all used strong blocks of colour in their paintings. They also chose unusual viewpoints and framed their images in surprising ways. Their paintings often have no single point of focus and the main subject is placed off centre. All of these characteristics can be found in Japanese prints.

Degas' points of view

Degas loved to experiment with unusual viewpoints and ways of framing his subjects. In his work, figures are often placed away from the centre of the picture to create a striking, asymmetrical composition. His paintings are also often framed so that part of a figure's arm or leg cannot be seen. These techniques have the effect of surprising the viewer, who is forced to look at a subject in a new way.

In the 1870s, Degas produced a series of studies of ballet dancers. Degas enjoyed showing the dancers from surprising viewpoints. Sometimes he showed them from below, as if they were being seen from the orchestra pit, and sometimes he showed them from above, as if he were watching them from a box in the theatre.

Pierre-Auguste Renoir, *The First Outing* (1876–77). In this painting of a young girl at the theatre, Renoir has made some very bold composition choices. Notice how the face of girl on the right is almost hidden from view!

Renoir's techniques

Like Japanese artists, Renoir enjoyed the contrast of different colours and patterns. He also experimented with framing his subjects in dramatic ways. In some of his paintings, a figure, such as a theatre-goer, is shown surprisingly close up, but cropped so that only a part of them can be seen.

This framing has the effect of drawing the viewer into the picture, so the viewer looks beyond the figure into the rest of the scene.

Cassatt's style

Cassatt was born in the United States, but spent most of her youth in France. In 1866, at the age of 22, she moved to Paris where she became a friend of Degas. Like Degas, she usually created asymmetrical compositions with unusual viewpoints. Cassatt was strongly influenced by Japanese art, and created her own prints in a deliberately Japanese style.

In the frame
Try framing an image in an unusual way. Cut out some cardboard frames of different sizes and place them over photos or pictures in magazines. You can produce some striking images simply by cutting off part of a figure. Try to create an interesting asymmetrical composition by positioning the main subject to one side of the picture.

Mary Cassatt, *Feeding the Ducks* (1895). Like the Japanese prints that she admired, Cassatt's prints have a flat, decorative quality, with areas of contrasting colour and pattern. Cassatt often takes an unusual viewpoint, and deliberately places her subjects off centre.

Impressionist subjects

The Impressionists established a new set of "subjects" for art. Unlike the artists favoured by the Paris Salon, the Impressionists did not paint scenes from history, the Bible, or mythology. Instead, they chose to concentrate on what they saw around them, and show subjects from modern life.

Impressionist artists painted scenes of the countryside, but also city streets and parks, and even railway stations. They showed people at work and at leisure, and they often used their own family and friends as their subjects.

Monet at Giverny

For the last 40 years of his life, Monet lived at Giverny, north-east of Paris. There he constructed a set of water gardens, inspired by the gardens of Japan. Monet made hundreds of paintings of his gardens at Giverny, often featuring a small wooden bridge and a lily pond. In the final years of his life, when his eyesight was failing, he produced a series of giant paintings of the surface of the pond, scattered with water lilies.

Claude Monet, *Haystack (Snow Effect)* (1891). Monet painted 25 views of haystacks, over a period of nine months. In these studies, he was especially interested in the light reflected by the haystack and the changing shapes and colours of the haystack's shadow.

Familiar landscapes

The Impressionists are famous for their landscapes. In their later years, Pissarro, Cézanne, and Sisley all settled in the French countryside, and devoted most of their time to painting the local villages, farms, and fields.

Pissarro painted views of his village of Pontoise. Sisley showed the small town of Louveciennes, often using a tree-lined road as the point of focus for his composition. Cézanne showed the hills and woods of Provence, a region in southern France, dominated by the rocky peak of Mont Sainte-Victoire. All of these artists painted the same scenes over and over again. In each painting they tried to capture different impressions of a familiar landscape.

Changing light and weather

The Impressionists were fascinated by the effects of light and weather on buildings and the natural landscape. They often painted the same scene at different times of year, or at different times of day.

In the summer of 1890, Monet began work on a series of paintings, showing haystacks in a field at different times of day and in different seasons. Later, he painted another series, showing the west front of Rouen Cathedral in different kinds of light. The many surfaces of the ancient stone building seemed to alter at different times, showing the changing effects of sunlight and shadows.

Try it yourself

Changing light
You can make your own study of the changing effects of light and weather. Take a series of photographs of the same scene at different times of day or in different weather conditions. The photos could be of a tree, bush, or small building – anything that casts a clear shadow.

Try mounting your photos in a series to show the changing effects of the light and shadows.

City life

The Impressionists were not just interested in country landscapes. They also aimed to capture a sense of life in Paris and its suburbs. Impressionist artists showed people strolling down the city streets and gathering in parks, cafés, and bars. The city's new railway stations also inspired many Impressionist images.

People at play

The Impressionists painted lively scenes of people enjoying their leisure in the city. Renoir's *The Ball at the Moulin de la Galette* shows a summer party in a working-class area of Paris. The people in the picture are all young working people, dressed up in their best clothes for a night out.

When the painting was first exhibited in 1877, many people were surprised that the artist had chosen to celebrate a social group that was not usually seen as a suitable subject for a painting.

One of Manet's most famous paintings of city life is *A Bar at the Folies-Bergère*. It shows a scene in a popular Paris nightspot. The painting's central subject is a young barmaid, with the scene in the bar reflected in the mirror behind her. The painting is remarkable for its inventive composition, but also because the main figure is a barmaid rather than a grand person from aristocratic society.

Pierre-Auguste Renoir, *The Ball at the Moulin de la Galette* (1876). The painting shows the artist's local café, and includes several of his young friends.

Édouard Manet, *Monet in his Floating Studio* (1874). In the summer of 1874, Manet visited Monet in Argenteuil. He painted several scenes of people boating on the river, including this portrait of Monet in his specially converted boat.

Out of town

The Impressionists often showed people enjoying a weekend in the country, spending a day by the river, or taking a trip to the seaside.

In the 1870s, Monet lived at Argenteuil, on the River Seine, a popular destination for day-trippers from Paris. He often invited his fellow artists to join him there, and paint people bathing and boating. Monet even converted a boat into a floating studio so that he could view life on the river from really close up.

Railway scenes

By the 1860s, steam trains were an important part of modern life. Railway trains, tracks, bridges, and stations all feature in the Impressionists' work. Monet, Manet, and Caillebotte all produced paintings of the busy Saint-Lazare railway station, and Monet painted the station 12 times. Monet's paintings convey a sense of grandeur and excitement, as the bustling figures of the passengers are dwarfed by the massive engines, and tall billows of steam fill the vast glass canopy of the station.

The world of entertainment

The world of entertainment held a powerful attraction for some of the Impressionists. Degas, Renoir, and Cassatt made regular visits to the Paris Opéra, to watch ballets and opera performances. Degas also liked to visit the circus and paint the daring tricks of the trapeze artists.

Edgar Degas, *Blue Dancers* (c.1899). This pastel study of ballet dancers catches them at a moment when they are totally absorbed in their own thoughts. As in many of Degas' pictures, the viewpoint and framing are very unusual.

Degas' dancers

Degas painted ballet dancers performing on stage as well as behind the scenes. Many of his paintings show dancers waiting in the wings, ready to go on stage. He also made a large number of studies of ballet dancers practising their steps in their rehearsal rooms. Some of Degas' studies of dancers rehearsing are finished paintings but many are drawn in pastels. Using pastels allowed Degas to work very fast and capture the dancers' movements.

Watching the audience

Renoir concentrated on the audience at the theatre, showing finely dressed women with their male companions (see page 24). Another keen observer of the theatre audience was Cassatt. In her painting *Two Young Ladies in a Loge*, she shows two young girls on their first outing to the theatre. The picture is a very sensitive portrait of the girls' combination of excitement and shyness.

People at work

The Impressionists did not only show people at play. Degas worked on a series of pictures of women working in hat shops. He also painted women ironing clothes and these studies convey a powerful sense of the women's weariness and exhaustion. Pissarro painted butchers in a market, while Manet showed men mending the road in a Paris street. These pictures of everyday, unglamorous work broke new ground for artists.

Degas at the races

The world of horse racing was a major theme in the paintings of Degas. He often attended race meetings, where he mingled with the crowds and watched the jockeys preparing for their races. Instead of painting the race itself, he preferred to concentrate on the horses and jockeys during the moments before and after the race. His paintings also show the spectators enjoying their day out.

Try it yourself

Watching the watchers

When people are busy watching an entertainment, they make excellent subjects for a picture. Why not try photographing or sketching your friends and family while they are watching television? You can create an interesting picture if you concentrate on their faces, but also show part of the room behind them.

The main focus of your picture should be the face of the person you are drawing. Just sketch in a few details of the room in the background.

Family and friends

The Impressionists rarely painted formal portraits, but their work is full of images of family and friends. Painters often showed their fellow artists at work, usually sitting in the open air with their easels and paints. They also painted many pictures of the women and children in their lives. In particular, the female members of the movement concentrated on women and children in their paintings.

Berthe Morisot, *The Butterfly Hunt* (1874). Morisot often painted mothers and children having fun out of doors – sitting by the river, chasing butterflies, or playing hide and seek in the bushes.

A female point of view

The two leading female Impressionist artists were Morisot and Cassatt. They were both extremely talented painters, who played a key role in the movement. Both artists used their roles as mothers and aunts as an opportunity to paint many images of mothers with children. One of Morisot's best-known works is *The Cradle*, which shows her sister Edma watching over her sleeping baby. *The Cradle* is a rather serious painting, but Morisot's studies of women and children usually show them in a relaxed and playful mood.

Cassatt painted many scenes of women at home with young children and babies. She also depicted the world of polite social visits. In a painting simply called *Tea*, Cassatt shows two very young women seated on a sofa, with a pot of tea in front of them. One of the women, the visitor, sips demurely from her cup, while the hostess looks restless and bored.

Mother and son

Monet often painted his wife Camille and their young son Jean. One of his most famous images of his wife and son is *The Stroll*. The picture was painted in 1875, when Jean was eight years old. It shows the mother and son on a grassy hill, on a bright, windy day. Camille is holding a green parasol.

Eleven years later, Monet painted another picture of a woman holding a parasol on a hill. By that time, Camille had died, and Monet used the daughter of a friend as his model. The colours are almost the same as in the earlier picture, but the woman's face has no features. Perhaps this was because Monet intended her to represent his dead wife, Camille.

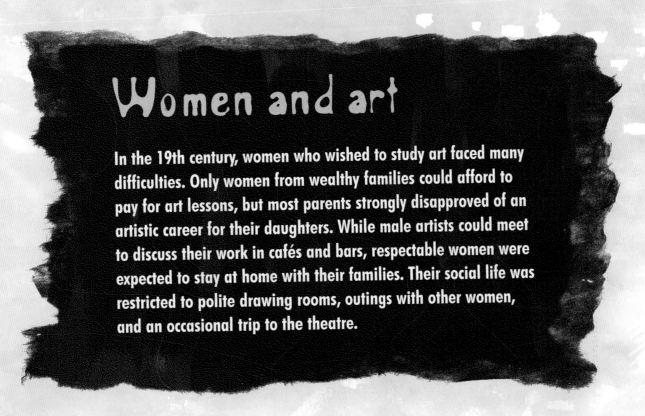

Women and art

In the 19th century, women who wished to study art faced many difficulties. Only women from wealthy families could afford to pay for art lessons, but most parents strongly disapproved of an artistic career for their daughters. While male artists could meet to discuss their work in cafés and bars, respectable women were expected to stay at home with their families. Their social life was restricted to polite drawing rooms, outings with other women, and an occasional trip to the theatre.

Making an Impression

By the 1890s, the influence of the Impressionists had spread from France to other countries in Europe and had also reached the United States and Australia. Artists outside France began to paint in the Impressionist style. The Impressionists also had an influence on music and literature.

Impressionists in the United States

In 1886 an exhibition of Impressionist paintings was held in New York and the new style was soon adopted by U.S. artists. One of the first U.S. artists to paint in the Impressionist style was Theodore Robinson. Robinson lived in France for eight years and beame a close friend of Monet. In 1892 Robinson returned to New York, where he taught art and helped to encourage the rapidly growing U.S. Impressionist movement.

From the 1890s until the 1920s, there were thriving groups of Impressionist artists in New England, Indiana, and California. Two other leading figures in the U.S. Impressionist movement were William Merritt Chase and Childe Hassam, who both went on to influence a new generation of artists.

Theodore Robinson, *Miss Motes and her Dog Shep* (1893). This painting was completed soon after Robinson returned from France to the United States. It clearly shows the influence of Robinson's friend, Monet.

Impressionists in Australia

In 1888 a group of landscape artists established a colony at Heidelberg, in the hills close to Melbourne, Australia. The group was led by Tom Roberts, who had visited France and had been inspired by the Impressionists. Roberts encouraged his artist friends to paint out of doors and to use an Impressionist style to capture the effects of light on the landscape. The Heidelberg School of artists included Arthur Streeton, Frederic McCubbin, and Charles Conder. Together, these artists pioneered a new way of showing the Australian landscape, producing pictures that were filled with a brilliant light and a sense of vast, open spaces.

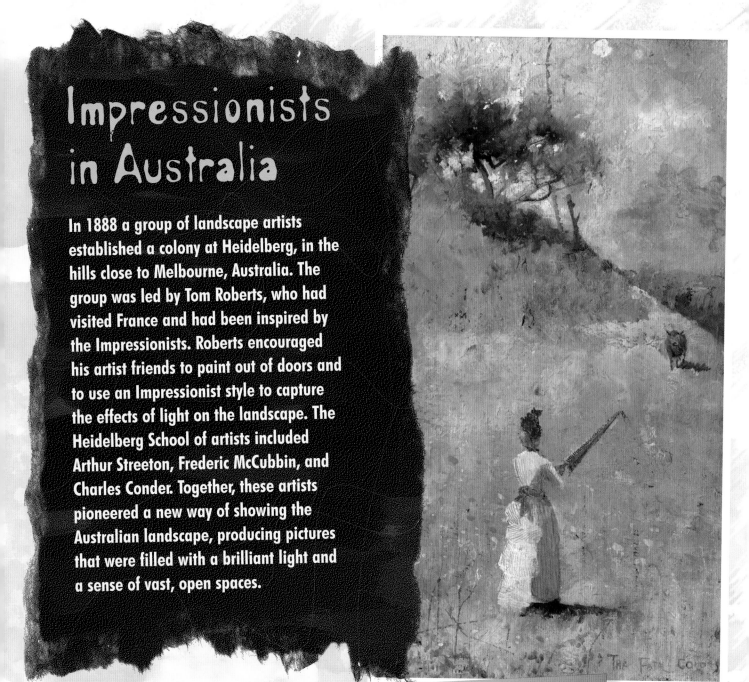

Charles Conder, *The Fatal Colour* (1888). Conder was born in England but settled in Australia in 1884. He soon became well known for his gently humorous paintings. In this painting, a fashionable lady is menaced by a bull, which is attracted by the "fatal colour" of her bright red parasol.

Whistler and the Impressionists

The U.S. artist James Abbot McNeill Whistler is sometimes described as an Impressionist, although he never considered himself to be one of the group. As early as the 1870s, he was painting landscapes that were strongly "impressionistic". Whistler's set of **nocturnes** represented misty scenes with just a few daringly simple strokes of paint.

The young Monet was greatly impressed by Whistler's paintings, and for a while he copied Whistler's style. His painting *Impression: Sunrise* (see page 18) shows the influence of Whistler's style.

British Impressionists

Impressionism was slow to spread to the United Kingdom. Most British artists found the Impressionists' work too sketchy. However, there were some exceptions to this response. Walter Sickert studied with Whistler in London and was a great admirer of Degas. He shared Degas' love of subjects from modern life and made a series of paintings of London music halls.

Another English Impressionist was Philip Wilson Steer. His scenes of children at the seaside clearly display the influence of Monet. In Scotland, James Guthrie and John Lavery both painted for a time in the Impressionist style, producing pictures of picnic outings and tennis games.

Music, novels, and poetry

Impressionism had an impact on other art forms. In 1887 Claude Debussy, a young French composer, wrote a piece called *Le Printemps* (The Spring), which aimed to create an impression of spring through a series of loosely linked "sound pictures". He also wrote a set of nocturnes, which he said were partly inspired by Whistler's paintings.

Some adventurous poets and novelists experimented with an "impressionistic" style of writing. Rather than describing things exactly, they used small details to convey impressions of a scene or things in the imagination. One of the best-known writers in this style was the English novelist Virginia Woolf.

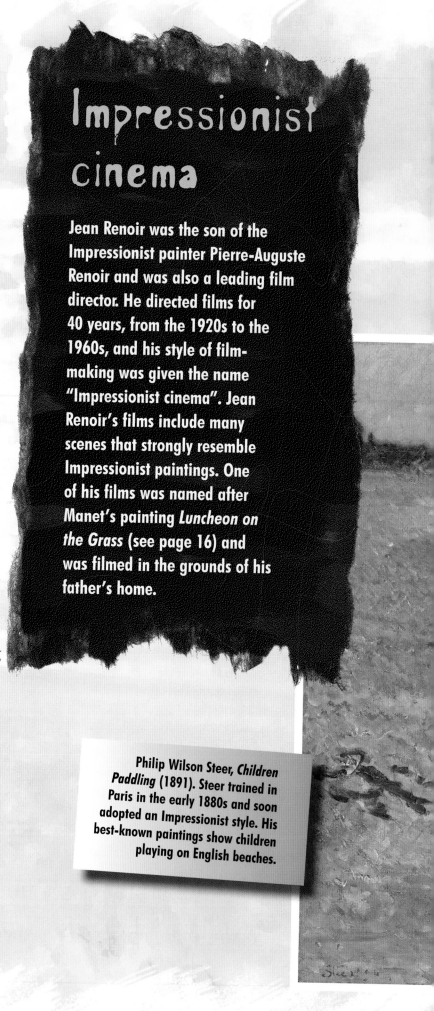

Impressionist cinema

Jean Renoir was the son of the Impressionist painter Pierre-Auguste Renoir and was also a leading film director. He directed films for 40 years, from the 1920s to the 1960s, and his style of film-making was given the name "Impressionist cinema". Jean Renoir's films include many scenes that strongly resemble Impressionist paintings. One of his films was named after Manet's painting *Luncheon on the Grass* (see page 16) and was filmed in the grounds of his father's home.

Philip Wilson Steer, *Children Paddling* (1891). Steer trained in Paris in the early 1880s and soon adopted an Impressionist style. His best-known paintings show children playing on English beaches.

Impressionist sculpture

Is there such a thing as Impressionist sculpture? Certainly, the Impressionist artists Degas and Renoir both created sculptures as well as paintings. Degas sculpted models of young dancers and Renoir produced a series of heads and figures. However, both of these artists turned to sculpture towards the end of their artistic careers, when they were moving away from an Impressionist style.

Most art critics agree that the sculptures of Degas and Renoir cannot be described as "impressionistic".

Some art critics believe that the Impressionist style had some influence on the work of the French sculptor Auguste Rodin. They have commented that the roughly worked surfaces of Rodin's sculptures, reflecting light in many directions, resemble the surfaces of Impressionist paintings.

After the Impressionists

By the late 1880s, the Impressionist group had lost its earlier unity, and artists within the group had begun to develop in different directions. Meanwhile, some artists had become critical of the Impressionist style. However, even the artists who reacted against Impressionism used the work of the Impressionists as a starting point from which to develop their own style of painting.

New directions

By the time of the last Impressionist exhibition in 1886, most of the artists within the Impressionist movement had begun to experiment with new, individual styles. Renoir and Degas concentrated on representing the human form, and their later paintings became more realistic in style. Meanwhile Monet explored decorative patterns in his work, especially in his studies of water lilies. In the 1880s, Cézanne became fascinated with the structure underlying his paintings, developing a style that would later be known as **Post-Impressionism**. At the same time, Pissarro began to experiment with **Neo-Impressionism**.

Post-Impressionism

Around 1885, a group of young painters, including Paul Gauguin and Vincent van Gogh, began to develop a dramatic new style. They used very strong outlines and vivid colours that sometimes bore no relation to the actual colours of the objects or scenes they were painting. This style of painting was given the name of Post-Impressionism – a title that included several styles of art, including the later work of Cézanne.

Even though the Post-Impressionists broke away from the Impressionists, they still built on the innovative style of the older artists. It was the Impressionists who had taken the first important steps towards new ways of using brushwork and colour.

Impressionist revival

In the first half of the 20th century, two French artists worked in a style that was very close to the work of the original Impressionists. Pierre Bonnard and Édouard Vuillard both produced paintings in an Impressionist style. Bonnard's series of paintings of his wife in the bath contain strong echoes of the work of Monet, Degas, and Renoir.

Paul Cézanne, *Mont Sainte-Victoire* (1902–04). With its strong geometric elements, this picture is typical of Cézanne's Post-Impressionist style. However, the influence of Impressionism can still be seen — both in the choice of colours and in the brushwork.

Neo-Impressionism

The work of the Impressionists was also the starting point for a distinctive style of art adopted by Seurat (see page 23). Seurat and his followers, including Paul Signac, painted their pictures using thousands of tiny coloured dots. This technique, sometimes known as pointillism, developed from the Impressionists' use of complementary colours. Pointillism is often known as Neo-Impressionism because it had its roots in the Impressionist movement.

The start of "modern art"

In the early years of the 20th century, art developed in many exciting new ways, but all these styles owed a debt to Impressionism. Through their daring use of colour, their discovery of new subjects, and their experiments with technique, the Impressionist artists broke away from traditional painting. The Impressionists depicted the world in a new and individual way, introducing the age of "modern art".

Lives of the artists

Paul Cézanne (1839–1906)

Cézanne grew up in Aix-en-Provence, in the south of France. He moved to Paris in 1861, where he soon met the other young Impressionists. Cézanne painted landscapes in Pointoise with Pissarro in the early 1870s, and exhibited at two Impressionist exhibitions. He later reacted against the Impressionist style and became one of the leading Post-Impressionists.

Gustave Caillebotte (1848–94)

Caillebotte came from a very wealthy Parisian family. He trained as a lawyer but later began to study painting. He soon became involved with the Impressionists and used his wealth to help fund their exhibitions and buy their paintings. Caillebotte's style is more realistic than that of most of the Impressionists, but he shared their interest in depicting scenes from modern city life. He showed his works at five of the eight Impressionist exhibitions.

Edgar Degas (1834–1917)

Degas was the son of a wealthy Paris banker. He had an academic art training but met Manet in 1862 and over the next few years began to paint works with modern-life themes. He contributed to seven of the eight Impressionist exhibitions. Degas specialized in scenes of theatres, cafés, and racecourses. In his later years, he mainly depicted ballet dancers and women bathing.

Mary Cassatt (1844–1926)

Cassatt was born in Pittsburg, USA. She was the daughter of a wealthy banker. In 1866 she moved to Paris and spent most of her adult life in France. She became a friend of Degas, and was invited by him to exhibit her works at the Impressionist exhibitions. Cassatt was an accomplished printmaker as well as a painter and was very interested in Japanese art. She is best known for her images of mothers and children.

Édouard Manet (1832–83)

Manet belonged to a wealthy Parisian family and trained as an academic painter. He was was one of the first 19th-century French artists to depict modern-life subjects. In the 1870s, he started to paint more out of doors, using lighter, brighter colours. Manet did not exhibit at any of the Impressionist exhibitions, but preferred to show his paintings at the Paris Salon.

Claude Monet (1840–1926)

Monet was the son of a grocer. He grew up in Le Havre in northern France, and as a young boy developed a talent for caricature. In 1858 he met the artist Eugène Boudin who taught him to paint landscapes. In the late 1860s, Monet played a very important part in developing the Impressionist style, along with Renoir. He showed works at five of the eight Impressionist exhibitions. In 1883 he moved to Giverny, where he lived for the rest of his life, producing hundreds of paintings of his water gardens.

Pierre-Auguste Renoir (1841–1919)

Renoir came from a poor family and he originally trained as a painter in a porcelain factory. He later played a significant part, alongside Monet, in creating the Impressionist style. Renoir is best known for his images of modern life in cafés and theatres, and for his paintings of women and young girls. He contributed to four of the Impressionist exhibitions, but in the 1880s he moved away from Impressionism and began to work in a more realistic style.

Berthe Morisot (1841–95)

Morisot came from a wealthy family. She studied with Corot and Manet and became an enthusiastic open-air painter. Morisot exhibited at seven of the eight Impressionist exhibitions. She married Manet's brother and had a daughter, Julie, who was the subject of many of her paintings. She specialized in domestic subjects, and is best known for her studies of women and children.

Alfred Sisley (1839–99)

Sisley had English parents but was born and brought up in Paris. He trained at Gleyre's studio with Monet and Renoir, and contributed to four of the Impressionist exhibitions. He concentrated on painting landscapes, and was especially praised for his treatment of skies.

Camille Pissarro (1830–1903)

Pissarro was born in the West Indies and settled in Paris in 1855. He was the only artist to show works in all eight of the Impressionist exhibitions. From 1872 to 1884, he lived in Pontoise, where he specialized in landscape painting. In 1885 he began to experiment with pointillism but returned to the Impressionist style in about 1890. He is best known for his country landscapes and his views of Paris.

Impressionism timeline

1840s Barbizon School artists pioneer the practice of painting landscapes in the open air

1850s French Realists begin to paint peasants working hard on the land, introducing the idea that the lives of the poor could be a suitable subject for art

1852 Napoleon III launches his campaign to modernize Paris, with new boulevards and railway stations that later inspire many Impressionist images

1854 Renoir trains as a porcelain painter

1855 Pissarro and Degas begin to study at the School of Fine Arts in Paris

1856 Degas leaves Paris for a three-year stay in Italy

1858 Monet meets Boudin in Normandy and Boudin introduces him to the practice of landscape painting in the open air

1859 Monet meets Pissarro in Paris

1860s Japanese prints become popular in Paris and influence some of the emerging Impressionist artists

1861 Cézanne moves to Paris and meets Pissarro

1862 Monet enters Gleyre's studio and there meets Renoir, Sisley, and Bazille; Manet paints *Music in the Tuileries Gardens* and meets Degas

1862–64 Monet leads open-air painting trips to the Forest of Fontainebleau to work with the Barbizon School artists

1863 The Salon des Refusés exhibition is held in Paris; Cézanne and Pissarro exhibit works at this exhibition, and Manet creates a scandal with his *Luncheon on the Grass*

1866 Cassatt arrives in Paris

1868 Manet meets Morisot; Monet, Renoir, Bazille, Sisley, and Degas begin to have regular meetings with Manet at the Café Guerbois in Paris; Pissarro and Cézanne also join the meetings occasionally

1869 Monet and Renoir paint at La Grenouillère, on the banks of the River Seine near Paris

1870 War breaks out between France and Prussia; Monet and Pissarro move to England, where they study the works of Constable and Turner and meet the art dealer Paul Durand-Ruel; Cassatt returns to the United States; Bazille is killed in action

1871	The Franco-Prussian war ends; Monet and Pissarro return to France; Monet moves to Argenteuil
1872	Pissarro settles in Pointoise, where he introduces Cézanne to painting out of doors
1873	Monet meets Caillebotte
1874	The first Impressionist exhibition is held in the photographer Nadar's studio in Paris; Monet exhibits *Impression: Sunrise*; an art critic gives the Impressionists their name; Cassatt returns to Paris
1876	Second Impressionist exhibition; Monet begins his series of paintings of the Saint-Lazare railway station
1877	Third Impressionist exhibition
1879	Fourth Impressionist exhibition, including works by Mary Cassatt
1880	Fifth Impressionist exhibition
1881	Sixth Impressionist exhibition
1882	Seventh Impressionist exhibition; Manet exhibits *A Bar at the Folies-Bergère* at the Salon
1883	Monet moves to Giverny

1885	Pissarro meets Seurat and begins to experiment with Neo-Impressionism; British-born Australian artist Tom Roberts returns to Australia from France and helps to introduce Impressionism to Australia, becoming the leading member of a group of artists known as the Heidelberg School
1886	Eighth and final Impressionist exhibition is held, including works by Gauguin, Seurat, and Signac, who later became known as Post-Impressionists; Van Gogh moves to Paris and meets Degas, Pissarro, and Gauguin; the art dealer Paul Durand-Ruel holds an exhibition of works by Impressionist artists in New York, USA
1892	U.S. artist Theodore Robinson returns to the United States from France and helps to encourage the rapidly growing U.S. Impressionist movement
1899	Monet begins his series of paintings of water lilies
1926	Monet, the last surviving major Impressionist, dies, bringing the movement to an end

Glossary

academic in art, a style of painting that originally developed in Italy in the 1500s. The style was characterized by realistic figure painting, close attention to detail, the use of fine brushwork, a smooth finish, and historical, mythological, or religious subject matter.

Academy of Fine Arts French society that organized an annual art exhibition in Paris, known as the Salon. The Academy encouraged artists to paint in the academic style, and favoured highly finished, realistic paintings, with historical, mythological, or religious themes.

art critic professional person who gives their opinion, often in a written review, about a work of art

art dealer person who buys and sells works of art

asymmetrical composition painting composition that is not balanced or symmetrical on either side of the centre

Barbizon School group of French landscape painters who worked in the village of Barbizon, on the outskirts of the forest of Fontainebleau in France. The artists were active from the 1830s until the 1870s and pioneered the practice of painting out of doors, directly in front of their subject, rather than in studios.

canvas strong, heavy woven piece of cloth used as a surface for oil paintings

caricature picture of a person, in which the person's features are exaggerated or distorted for comic effect

colour wheel way of arranging the primary colours (blue, red, and yellow) and the secondary colours (orange, green, and purple) to show their relationship. Colours that are opposite each other on the circle are called complementary colours.

commercial to do with business and making a profit

complementary colours colours that are opposite each other on the colour wheel (e.g., red and green, yellow and purple, blue and orange). The complementary of a primary colour is made by mixing the other two primary colours (e.g., the complementary of red is green, which is made by mixing yellow and blue). When they are used next to each other, complementary colours appear more intense.

composition arrangement of the different elements or subjects in a painting

flat colour solid, unbroken, single colour

Franco-Prussian War war fought by France against Prussia and the other German states, from 1870 to 1871. The French Army was defeated and the war resulted in the overthrow of Emperor Napoleon III.

French Realists group of artists who emerged in the mid-19th century and aimed to show subjects realistically, as they appeared in everyday life, rather than in an idealized way

Impressionist exhibitions series of eight public art exhibitions held in Paris between 1874 and 1886, showing works by Impressionist artists

Impressionist movement movement in painting that began in France in the 1860s and lasted until the early 20th century. Impressionist artists aimed to capture their impressions of the effects of light and colour in nature. The movement undermined the status of the style of art favoured by the French Academy of Fine Arts and paved the way for modern art movements in the 20th century.

Industrial Revolution rapid expansion of industry that began in the United Kingdom in the mid-18th century, and in the 19th century spread throughout Europe and to the United States

innovative original and creative

landscape painting painting of a view of natural scenery

Neo-Impressionism late 19th-century movement in French painting led by Seurat and Signac, who created paintings using pointillist techniques

nocturne in music, a short romantic composition, often written for the piano; in art, a painting of a night scene

optical mixing process by which the eyes and brain of the viewer mix two colours together when they are placed side by side

optics scientific study of sight and the behaviour of light

palette choice of colours used in an artist's work

palette knife blade with a handle for mixing colours and applying paint

plein-air painting painting out of doors in the open air

pointillism technique in which paint is applied in dots of colour. When viewed from a distance, the dots appear to merge together and the colours appear brighter and more intense.

point of focus the part of a painting that the eye naturally focuses on

Post-Impressionism term used to describe the work of artists who broke away from the Impressionist style and developed their own individual styles. Leading Post-Impressionist artists include Cezanne, Gauguin, Seurat, and Van Gogh.

primary colours colours – red, blue, and yellow – that cannot be made from a mixture of other colours

Salon France's official art exhibition, first held in 1667. Paintings included in the exhibition were chosen by a jury made up of members of the French Academy of Fine Arts, who favoured academic-style paintings.

Salon des Refusés art exhibition held in 1863, which showed paintings that had been rejected by the official Salon that year, including Manet's *Luncheon on the Grass*

social relating to the way a society is organized and how people live in the society

studio artist's workroom

subject figure or scene depicted by an artist

taches short, small dabs of separate colour

woodblock print block of wood that is cut or carved so that an image is left in relief. Coloured ink is then applied to the raised image and the image is pressed against paper to create a print.

Find out more

Useful websites

General sites on Impressionism, with examples of Impressionist works

www.artlex.com
An online art dictionary. Click on "Im" to find information on Impressionism and links to pages showing examples of works by individual artists.

www.artchive.com/74nadar.htm
A virtual recreation of the first Impressionist exhibition in 1874, including images of catalogues and reviews.

www.ibiblio.org/wm/paint/glo/impressionism
An introduction to Impressionism, with links to information on all the major Impressionists and examples of their works.

www.impressionism.org
Click on "Experience Impressionism" for a fun guided tour, with examples of major Impressionist works and information on the concepts that defined the Impressionist movement.

www.museumsyndicate.com
An online gallery. Click on "Browse by artist" and scroll down to find examples of works by individual Impressionist artists.

www.nationalgallery.org.uk
The website of the National Gallery in London, UK. For an introduction to Impressionism and links to pages on the major Impressionist artists, click on "Collection", then "Collection features" and "The Impressionists".

www.nga.gov
The website of the National Gallery of Art in Washington, D.C. To tour the Impressionist collection, click on "The Collection", then scroll down to "Paintings" and click on "French 19th century".

Sites featuring individual artists

http://giverny.org/monet/welcome.htm
A site devoted to Claude Monet's life and work, including a section on Monet's garden at Giverny.

www.metmuseum.org
The website of the Metropolitan Museum of Art, New York. Click on "Explore & learn", and "Artists", to reach information on the life and works of Cassatt as well as an online tour "The Dancers and Degas".

www.nga.gov/onlinetours/index.shtm
For an online tour of the life and works of Boudin, from the National Gallery of Art, in Washington, D.C., click on "Eugène Boudin at the National Gallery of Art" under the "Artists" menu. Click on "Edgar Degas" under the "Artists" menu for an online tour entitled "The Dance Lesson", which explores Degas' paintings of ballet dancers.

British Impressionism

www.tate.org.uk
To view a collection of paintings by British Impressionists, from the Tate Gallery, UK, click on "Tate Collection", then "Explore by subject", and type "British Impressionism" into the search bar.

French Realism

www.musee-orsay.fr/en/home.html
Information from the Musée d'Orsay, France, on Courbet and French Realism. Click on "Collections" and then "Courbet Dossier".

U.S. Impressionists

www.nga.gov
The website of the National Gallery of Art in Washington, D.C. To see works by major U.S. Impressionist artists, click on "The Collection", then scroll down to "Paintings" and click on "American". From here you can select the online tour "American Impressionists of the Late 1800s and Early 1900s".

www.metmuseum.org
The site of the Metropolitan Museum of Art, New York. Click on "Explore and learn", and "Artists", to reach information on Mary Cassatt and Childe Hassam.

More books to read

Impressionism (Art Revolutions), by Linda Bolton (Belitha Press, 2003)

Impressionism: Art, Leisure and Parisian Society, by Robert L. Herbert (Yale University Press, 1991)

How to Paint Like the Impressionists, by Susie Hodge (Collins, 2004)

Impressionism (Art and Ideas), by James Henry Rubin (Phaidon Press, 1999)

Impressionism: Origins, Practice, Reception (World of Art), by Belinda Thomson (Thames & Hudson, 2000)

Paint with the Impressionists: A Step-by-Step Guide to Their Methods and Materials for Today's Artists, by Jonathan Stephenson (Thames & Hudson, 1995)

The Impressionists at Leisure, by Pamela Todd (Thames & Hudson, 2007)

Other artists to research

Why not extend your studies and find out about some other less well-known Impressionist artists, either by searching the Internet, or by looking in books?

Less well-known French Impressionists who showed works at the Impressionist exhibitions include Armand Guillaumin, Marie Bracquemond, and Jean-Louis Forain. Other U.S. Impressionist artists you might find out about include Frederick Carl Frieseke, Willard Metcalf, John Henry Twachtman, and J. Alden Weir. Less well-known British Impressionists include William McTaggart. You might also investigate the Australian group of Impressionist artists known as the "Heidelberg School".

Index